by Meish Goldish
illustrated by Sean O'Neill

SCHOOL PUBLISHERS

Printed in China

ISBN 10: 0-15-351677-1
ISBN 13: 978-0-15-351677-1

Ordering Options
ISBN 10: 0-15-351215-6 (Grade 5 Advanced Collection)
ISBN 13: 978-0-15-351215-5 (Grade 5 Advanced Collection)
ISBN 10: 0-15-358160-3 (package of 5)
ISBN 13: 978-0-15-358160-1 (package of 5)

5 6 7 8 9 10   468   12 11 10 09

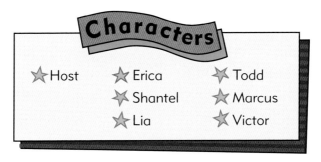

Host: Good afternoon, home viewers. Welcome to our program, *Community Helpers.* Each week, we talk to kids from our area who have improved the town in some way. Today we've got some enterprising students from Clearview Elementary School. Let's find out what they did. What is your name?

Erica: Hi, I'm Erica. I'm part of "Kids Cleaning Up".

Host: What kind of group is that?

Erica: We're a student advocacy group that fights pollution.

3

Host: What do you do to fight pollution?

Erica: At Clearview, we started a program to promote the three R's. That's *recycle, reduce,* and *reuse.* We watched what students did with their trash. We detected a big problem. Too many kids weren't recycling their plastic juice containers and glass bottles. They were tossing them into garbage cans with all the other trash. That's not helpful.

Host: Why is it important to recycle?

Erica: Are you kidding? Recycling is a vital activity. All those bottles add up. Soon you've got a mountain of bottles! Also, our town is running out of landfills. Those are the places where trash is buried.

Host: What's the solution?

Erica: "Kids Cleaning Up" tries to get all students to recycle. We put up posters around our school. They explain how glass and plastic are reused to make other products. Glass and plastic can be recycled instead of buried.

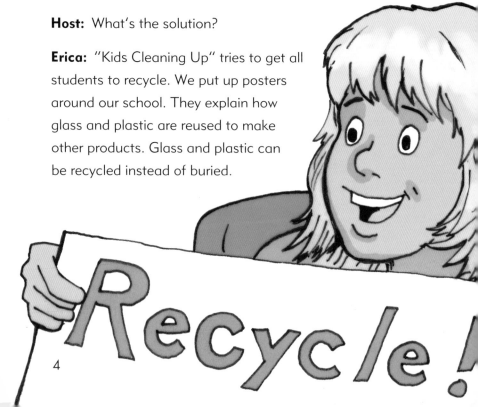

Host: Isn't the same true of paper?

Erica: I'll let Todd answer that. He's our paper expert.

Todd: Thank you. Yes, recycling paper is very important. We've mistreated our forests by cutting down too many trees. If we recycle paper, we can save more trees. Remember, many animals live in trees, from birds to ants. We should be more compassionate. We shouldn't destroy their homes. After all, a tree is an animal's castle.

Host: Are trees helpful in other ways as well?

Todd: Yes, they are. The leaves provide us with shade on hot days. They also produce oxygen, which we all need to breathe.

Host: Are other parts of a tree important?

Todd: The roots hold our soil together, so after a heavy rain, the ground doesn't just wash away. Be thankful for that!

Host: How do you recycle paper at Clearview?

Todd: We've placed boxes and waste cans all around the school. They're labeled "Recycled Paper Only." Students drop in any papers they no longer need, like old homework or newspapers. That paper gets recycled into new sheets of paper.

Host: What else are you doing?

Todd: We encourage reusing as well as recycling. We urge our students to find new uses for old papers. For example, they might use old magazine pictures to make birthday cards for friends and family.

Host: What a wonderful idea!

Todd: Thank you. We also donate old magazines to hospitals. You'd be surprised how people there really appreciate them. "Kids Cleaning Up" wants to create a paper sensibility and, at the same time, a sense of altruism in students.

Host: It sounds like you're succeeding. Now let's move on to another member of your group.

Shantel: Hi, I'm Shantel. I'm here to talk about reducing.

Host: I guess I could stand to stop spending money.

Shantel: Oh, I'm not talking about spending money. I'm talking about lessening the amount of trash we make.

Host: How is reducing different from recycling and reusing?

Shantel: Recycling and reusing are ways of using trash again. Reducing is creating less trash to begin with.

Host: Can you give us an example?

Shantel: Okay, suppose you take an excursion to the toy store. You see two different jump ropes. One comes in a box with a large plastic cover. The other rope is coiled and wrapped in a small paper seal. Which one would you buy?

Host: Hmmm, I never thought about that before. Which jump rope should I buy?

Shantel: Pick the one with the small paper seal. The other rope comes in a sleek box, but it's all just trash the moment you tear it open.

Host: You're saying that I can reduce my trash by buying the rope with the simpler packaging.

Shantel: Exactly! Now, I'm not saying companies should sell their products in dilapidated, damaged packages. I'm saying they should make as little trash as possible.

Host: Can you suggest another way to reduce?

Shantel: Suppose you go to the grocery store for a few items. Bring along your own cloth sack. That way, you won't need to use the store's plastic or paper bags. You'll have no trash to throw away. Also, you can reuse your cloth sack later.

Host: "Kids Cleaning Up" is full of good ideas! What else have you done?

Shantel: Wait until you hear what Marcus did!

Marcus: I'm just bursting to tell you! I've been the giddiest student at Clearview all week. Some kids think it's impossible to bring about change in our school, but I proved it can be done.

Host: What, exactly, did you do?

Marcus: Well, I noticed that our school cafeteria was using plastic cups, not paper cups. Our teacher taught us that plastic takes a longer time to break down in the earth than paper.

Host: You mean when it's buried as trash?

Marcus: That's right. Anyway, I asked a cafeteria worker whether we could start using paper cups in the cafeteria instead.

Host: What did she tell you?

Marcus: The worker said she wasn't in charge of buying the cups. She told me to talk to the cafeteria manager.

Host: What happened?

Marcus: He told me to talk to his boss. She told me to talk to the school principal.

Host: It sounds like you had to do a lot of walking.

Marcus: I hustled and bustled like a rocket! I wound up talking to the head of the whole school district.

Host: What did you say?

Marcus: I explained why we should be using paper cups instead of plastic and how little changes like that can add up. The head of schools agreed with me. She said she was impressed with my concern. As a result, now every school in our district uses paper cups, not plastic. The paper doesn't make the drinks taste bland either.

Host: That's a great story! I still want to get to our last guests before we run out of time. What is your name?

Lia: My name is Lia, and I'm also part of "Kids Cleaning Up". I help run a special program at Clearview.

Host: What kind of program is it?

Lia: It's really more like a contest. Every grade in our school takes part. At the end of each day, we collect all the trash from all the grades. We weigh each container of paper, plastic, glass, metal, and regular trash.

Host: That must take a lot of coordination.

Lia: Yes, many students are involved. We collect and weigh each kind of trash. Then we make sure the janitors throw all of it away.

Host: Why do you weigh each grade's trash?

Lia: It's part of our contest. We call it "Trash Diet." At the end of each week, we add up how many pounds of trash each grade made. We give out certificates to the winners. There's "Least Paper," "Least Glass," and so on. Once a month, we give out small prizes to the grade with the "Least Total Trash."

Host: Where do the prizes come from?

Lia: Local stores donate them. They've been very generous so far. It's a great way to get students to go on a trash diet.

Host: I hope the prizes aren't packaged in a lot of extra wrapping. That would only add to your trash!

Lia: You're right! We loathe trash and want to set a good example for others. If we are good mentors, then other kids will pick up our good habits.

Host: Now we have one final guest. Who are you?

Victor: I'm Victor. I educate the public about pollution.

Host: Tell us some of the things you've done.

Victor: Well, I've written many letters. Clearview students take them home to their parents. I suggest ways that parents can cut down on pollution. For example, they should walk or bike when possible instead of using their cars. Car fumes add to our air pollution.

Host: That's true. I prefer to bask in the sun.

Victor: That's nice, but you've got to be careful when doing that, too. In the sky, there's a layer of air called ozone. It's supposed to block out the sun's harmful rays, but over the years, the ozone layer has been weakened. If you sit in the sun, you should use sunscreen to protect your skin.

Host: How has the ozone layer been weakened?

Victor: People sprayed a lot of chemicals into the air. They came from aerosol cans for things like deodorant sprays, hair sprays, and air fresheners.

Host: How can we reduce the air pollution caused by the cans?

Victor: Actually, a lot has already been done. Many companies have stopped using harmful chemicals in their sprays. However, there's still more we can do. For example, I myself use a roll-on deodorant instead of a spray.

Host: That's good thinking. It's clear that "Kids Cleaning Up" has a lot of good ideas. You're also full of fervor for your cause. You truly believe in it. Would any of you care to leave our viewers with a final piece of advice?

Erica: Recycle, reuse, and reduce!

Todd: Fight against pollution!

Host: Those are good words to live by. Good-bye, everyone!

14

Think Critically

1. Summarize this Readers' Theater in a few sentences.

2. What does Marcus mean when he says, "I'm just bursting to tell you"?

3. How can you tell that the members of "Kids Cleaning Up" care about their work?

4. Would you want to be a member of "Kids Cleaning Up"? Why or why not?

5. What do you think is the author's purpose in writing this Readers' Theater?

 **Language Arts**

Write a Letter Suppose Victor asked you to write a letter to school parents. In your letter, suggest several ways that adults might cut down on pollution in the community and the world. Make your letter as persuasive as possible.

School-Home Connection Summarize the story for family members. Then ask them to suggest ways to make our planet a cleaner place to live.

Word Count: 1,607